THE RED BOOK OF
Luck

THE RED BOOK OF
Luck

Amy Treadwell

CHRONICLE BOOKS
SAN FRANCISCO

Library of Congress Cataloging-in-Publication Data available.
ISBN 978-1-4521-6975-0

Manufactured in China

Illustrations by Vikki Chu

10 9 8 7 6 5 4 3 2 1

Velcro is a registered trademark of Velcro BVBA.

Chronicle books and gifts are available at special quantity discounts to
corporations, professional associations, literacy programs, and other organizations.
For details and discount information, please contact our corporate/premiums
department at corporatesales@chroniclebooks.com or at 1-800-759-0190.

Chronicle Books LLC
680 Second Street
San Francisco, California 94107
www.chroniclebooks.com

"Nothing is as obnoxious as other people's luck."

— *F. Scott Fitzgerald*

CONTENTS

INTRODUCTION

Luck, kismet, serendipity, fate, superstition—call it what you will, but every culture around the globe believes in it and has developed countless symbols, objects, gestures, and actions all designed to improve it.

The simple fact is that our lives are not always under our control, and when good or bad things happen we often credit luck as the source. Sometimes luck "happens," and sometimes it's a very specific gesture or sequence that we believe will get us the new job or help us win the lottery. Many of these rituals have origins that go back to pagan times, while others have been born of the moment and are stuck to until they stop working (think baseball players).

Whether you believe in luck or not, the concept is tied to nearly every aspect of our lives, and the stories of where they come from can be fascinating. From lucky objects and charms to lucky colors and numbers, everything you ever wanted to know about luck is right here. How lucky can you get?

CHAPTER 1

LUCKY SYMBOLS

ACORNS

The oak tree is a symbol of Thor, the hammer-holding Norse god. In ancient times, acorns were collected and displayed somewhere inside the home to protect residents against lightning strikes. This ritual has evolved over time, and people today often carry an acorn in their pocket for good luck.

ANTS

If you find ants building a home near your front door, some say it's a sign that you will have financial security.

BAMBOO

Giving bamboo to someone else brings the receiver good luck. It's important to note that for maximum fêng shui, the number of stalks makes a difference. For general luck you need at least five stalks, but if you can get twenty-one stalks you will also receive good health and abundant wealth.

BASIL

This aromatic herb has many positive attributes, including love, wealth, beauty, and of course luck. It's also thought to be an antidepressant with antibacterial properties. If you need luck in your finances, grow some basil in your garden.

BASKETS

Meeting someone carrying full baskets is considered good luck, especially if you're on a journey. But if you cross paths with someone whose baskets are empty, it portends misfortune.

BATS

In Chinese culture, bats are a symbol of a long and happy life, and amulets or pendants of bats are often worn to protect against bad luck. Some legends say that bats only hang out in auspicious places, so it's lucky if they want to be near you. If your bat is red, even better, because red bats ward off evil.

BEARS

Bears are revered by some Native American tribes, Siberian clans, and indigenous people from the Alaskan territory. They are thought to have much power due to their size and ability to nourish themselves even during the long months of hibernation. They are a symbol of strength and survival, which is very auspicious.

BEES

It is unlucky to give away bees. If you need to get rid of a hive, it's best to sell it to someone for a price that

shows its worth. A woman who is about to be married should sell bees before the ceremony, to ensure a long and happy marriage. And if a bee enters your home, you will soon receive a visitor or have good luck. It's important that the bee leaves of its own accord to maintain that luck.

BEETLES

These were lucky for ancient Egyptians (who called them scarabs) because of their connection to the sun, which was relied upon in the right doses to grow their plants—not enough and nothing will grow, too much and the plants will wither and die. Beetles harness the sun by rolling their eggs in mud and using the sun to incubate them. They are a symbol of rebirth, and protect from evil.

BIRDS

If one flies into the house, it is a sign of good luck. When a bird calls from the west, you'll have good luck, but a call from the north is a precursor to tragedy. When a blackbird nests in your house, you will have a full year of good luck. Also see Doves, page 25.

BULLS

This is a very positive symbol in many cultures, from the Greeks and Egyptians to the Celts and East Indians. The bull embodies virility and strength as well as good health. If you wear the bull as a pendant, you will be blessed with a large family and generous crops.

CATS

Cats are thought to be both lucky and unlucky depending on the type of cat, what they are doing, and how you happen to come across one. The luck or lack of it can also change depending on the culture or country of origin. If the cat sneezes near you on your wedding day, you will have a happily married life. In Russia, some parents deliberately put a cat into their child's crib to ward off evil spirits. Finding a white hair on a black cat is supposed to bring good luck. It's also good luck to dream of a white cat, which will increase your creativity and awareness of the spirit. Dreams of a tortoiseshell

cat mean you'll be lucky in love. Dream of a ginger cat and your luck will lean toward success in money and business. In the United States, if a black cat crosses your path, that's a sign of bad luck, and if a white cat crosses your path that's good luck. But the opposite is true in the United Kingdom—seeing a white cat in your path is a sign of bad luck, and if a bride and groom run into a black cat on their wedding day, it's considered good luck and a sign of a long and happy marriage. And a French superstition claims that it's bad luck to cross a stream while carrying a cat.

CORNUCOPIA

This is a symbol of abundance and always having plenty. It is also thought to be able to ward off the evil eye.

CRICKETS

Because of its song, the cricket is considered a sign of protection. It will warn you if someone is close by stopping its chirping. A cricket on the hearth means the household will have good luck.

CROWS

The number of crows in a murder indicates various levels of luck based on this little rhyme:

One's bad
Two's luck
Three's health
Four's wealth
Five's sickness
Six's death

DOGS

Man's best friend is thought to help overcome obstacles and increase wealth and prosperity. According to folklore, it's good luck to meet a greyhound with a white spot or a Dalmatian, and coming across any dog while on a journey will bring you good fortune. If a strange black dog follows you home, you'll also be lucky. But if you walk by one as it starts to howl at the moon, that is a bad omen.

DOLPHINS

Sailors have thought of the dolphin as a symbol of luck since ancient times. If one was seen during a voyage, it meant land was close at hand.

DONKEYS

A very old saying claims "no one ever sees a dead donkey," so if you do see one it's considered good luck because it's so rare. And you can also bring about good luck by jumping over a dead donkey three times.

DOVES

In the Bible, a dove was the bearer of the olive branch that showed Noah that the floodwaters were receding. Doves are closely connected with love and the ancient Romans believed them to be the messengers of Venus. However, the dove is considered bad luck for miners, and miners often refused to go underground if they saw a dove fly near the mine shaft.

EGGS

In Britain, white eggs are often given for luck, but not brown ones, which are considered unlucky. Eggs are also believed to bring luck in fertility, increase virility, bring a bountiful harvest, and protect children from misfortune.

ELEPHANTS

In India, the elephant is a talisman of fortune, wealth, and luck. If wearing one on a pendant, the trunk should be worn upright for luck in business. The Hindu god Ganesha is in the form of an elephant and is the god of fortune and luck—having elephants around you is like having Ganesha watch out for your success.

FROGS

These are often associated with rain, which has been a symbol of luck since agricultural times. Frogs are also a lucky symbol of fertility, travel, and transformation, and a little clay "fortune frog" can be used as a good luck talisman to bring wealth and good fortune into the home. To get the best results, the frog should be placed on a red piece of paper, and make sure a coin is placed in its mouth.

GNOMES

Gnomes became synonymous with the cute little statues in millions of gardens worldwide. But their history goes way back to when they were thought to guard the treasures of the earth. Statues of gnomes in gardens have been around since the Renaissance and their popularity continues today, as they are believed to bring protection and good fortune.

GOLDFISH

The goldfish is one of the eight sacred symbols of the Buddha, and a Chinese symbol of fortune, wealth, and surplus. In ancient Egypt, people kept goldfish in their homes as a lucky charm to improve domestic relations. They are also lucky to give to friends to wish them a prosperous year.

HAWAIIAN TI PLANT

Early Polynesians felt this plant had mystical powers, so if you have one in your home, good fortune will come to all who reside there. If your plant has two stalks, you'll double your luck and also find love.

HEDGEHOGS

These are said to be lucky if you meet one going in the opposite direction.

HOLLY

A sprig of holly saved from holiday celebrations can be kept for luck and to keep evil spirits away during the year.

HONEYSUCKLE

Along with its lovely fragrance and sweet nectar, it is thought to offer protection and luck to the one who cares for it.

HORSESHOES

Legend has it that mischievous fairies can't get near iron, so people would make horseshoes with iron and nail them to their door or a wall in their house to keep fairies away. But be careful how you hang a horseshoe. If you

hang it with the ends pointing down, your luck may pour out, but if you hang it with the ends pointing up, you'll catch luck continuously. Finding one on your travels is always a good omen.

HORSES

Horses are a symbol of power, strength, and beauty. They have long been considered lucky because of their contributions to the success of battles. In bygone times, if you owned a horse you were considered high ranking, which would help you continue to prosper. The piebald horse in particular is good luck, but if you see his tail first bad luck will befall a friend.

JADE PLANT

Plants with rounded leaves are considered good luck, and the jade plant is a good example of such greenery. The jade plant is often given as a gift to new business owners, and if placed near the entrance is thought to bring success and prosperity.

JASMINE

For those who want to be lucky in love, grow jasmine. This intensely aromatic flower is one of the most powerful aphrodisiacs.

LADYBUGS

Some say if a ladybug lands on your arm and you let it sit there without shaking it off, your luck will get better. Farmers have thought that if there are a larger than usual number of ladybugs in springtime, there will be an abundant harvest that year. And the deeper red the ladybug is, the stronger the luck. Don't kill a ladybug, however, or bad luck will follow.

LIZARDS

If you are looking for good luck for vision or for protection from the unseen, the lizard is your talisman. They are nocturnal, so they see what happens while you are sleeping.

LOTUS

If you plant your garden with lotus, it will be filled with luck and purity. However, you must be sure to remove any wilted blooms or dead leaves to retain any luck.

MONEY TREE

Also called a Pachira, they are most often seen with their trunks braided together. If you want to be sure the plant will be lucky, the plant needs to have three or five braided trunks (no unlucky four, please). The leaves also need to have at least five fingers.

MOON

Some superstitions say that the moon is made of silver and if you see a full moon and then tap your wallet or purse, riches will come your way. During a full moon is an auspicious time to start a new job. The full moon is also thought to bring on sickness or even death, so don't sleep directly under one or look at one if you don't feel well—you might not get better.

MORNING GLORIES

Growing these is lucky because they bring peace and happiness. If you put the seeds under your pillow you will be free of nightmares.

PEACHES

Peaches are a symbol of longevity, happiness, and prosperity. In Korea, it is a very lucky fruit. However, it's believed that it will chase away spirits, so if you are honoring your ancestors, peaches should not be a part of the event.

PHOENIX

The phoenix is one of the four fêng shui animals (the dragon, tiger, and tortoise are the others, with the dragon and tiger representing strength and protection, while the tortoise offers luck). It provides a safe, harmonious, and prosperous home. The phoenix has the ability to take bad luck and convert it into good luck. In the fêng shui system, it is always red and sits directly below the dragon. When all four animals are in their proper positions, all will be well. Also see Tortoises, page 41.

PIGS

In China and in Ireland the pig is very auspicious. If you see a pig in clover it is particularly favorable and more money is soon to come your way. But seeing a pig right after you get married is bad luck.

RABBITS

A very common token of luck for fertility and childbirth, a rabbit is a harbinger of spring and is extremely lucky, particularly after a hard winter. They symbolize rebirth and renewal. But just like a black cat in the United States, having one cross your path can spell bad luck.

RAINBOWS

The most popular luck attached to rainbows is the belief that leprechauns hide their gold at the end of the rainbow, though, as it's impossible to ultimately reach the end of a rainbow, the luck attached is more about hope than about attaining riches.

RICE

Rice in the house will bring prosperity. To get the most luck from the rice, keep it in a deep ceramic container (symbolizing the deep pockets of a rich man) and be sure to put a few coins or money at the bottom of the container. Make sure it has a tight lid. Store it in a cabinet, preferably behind closed doors.

ROSES

Growing roses is thought to bring luck, healing, and love.

RUBBER PLANT

Like jade plants, these are lucky because of their round leaves.

SHAMROCKS

Shamrocks are also known as white clover. Despite the common thought that four-leaf clovers are lucky, the classic three-leaf shamrock also brings good tidings to the lucky holder. Some say each leaf has meaning—one means faith, one hope, the last love. And if you find the very rare four-leaf clover, that last leaf is considered the luckiest of all.

SNAKE PLANT

Also known as the mother-in-law's tongue, it became a symbol of luck because it can remove toxins like formaldehyde and benzene from the air.

SPIDERS

Spiders have been a sign of luck since Roman times. Wearing a spider symbol will draw success to you much like a spider's web draws in its prey.

TEA

Luck is said to be found in many ways through tea. In bygone times, there were those who, every morning, would swirl the dregs of their cup of tea to find out if their day would be good or bad. Some people think if you throw out tea leaves in front of your home, it will ward off evil. Others think if you drop tea leaves inside your home, it's lucky. It's unlucky for fisherman to finish a pot before they have finished fishing or the nets will always be empty. Their families also won't empty the pot when the fisherman goes out to prevent the ship from going down at sea.

TORTOISES

In the world of fêng shui, the lucky tortoise is collected with the tiger, dragon, and phoenix as one of four animals offering protection. If you place a picture of a tortoise at the back of your house you will have financial security and luck. Also see Phoenix, page 36.

WHEELS

The wheel, with its unending shape, is a symbol of good luck and moving forward. And the optimum luck comes from a wheel that can move in a clockwise direction, which is considered the ultimate auspicious direction for successful businesspeople.

CHAPTER 2

CHARMS AND GOOD FORTUNE

LUCKY TALISMANS

ANKH

In ancient Egypt, the ankh was considered the symbol of eternal life. Many people would wear it as a talisman, and the symbol was used repeatedly in paintings and art. It is also a sign of fertility, so it's popular with those wishing for a child or wanting to increase the size of their family.

AXE

Wearing an axe-head on a chain around your neck is thought to ensure that success will come you.

COINS

Finding pennies is supposed to bring a day's good fortune, but other coins can be auspicious as well. If you find a bent coin or one with a hole in it, that can be the most lucky. Carry it on a necklace around your neck or in your left pocket and you can supersize your luck. Other ways to gain luck from coins are to keep a jar of pennies on your kitchen counter, carry a coin made in your birth year or in a leap year in your pocket, and place a coin in a new purse or wallet to add a little more luck to your life.

DICE

Luck associated with dice started during World War II when pilots would bring any item they could find that might bring luck with them in their planes. Gambling items like playing cards and dice were popular items. After the war, an enterprising company started making fuzzy dice, which gained popularity as a lucky item to hang from the rearview mirrors of cars.

GUARDIAN BELL

One of the more modern signs of luck is the guardian bell that protects motorcycles and their riders. This small metal bell is hung under the motorcycle and sucks in evil spirts or gremlins. These negative spirits are thought to be the cause of any misfortune, personal or mechanical, that might befall a rider. It's considered even more protective if received as a gift. It works like this: The evil spirit is lured inside the bell and then driven crazy by the ringing. The only way out is down, so the evil spirit drops onto the road, creating potholes (bad luck for other motorcycles—unless they have a guardian bell).

KEY

One of the oldest lucky charms is the key, which has been traditionally given between women and men as a symbol of unlocking one's heart to love. Ancient Greeks and Romans thought it represented the Key of Life, which would unlock a door and pass on their prayers to the gods. In Japan, if you tie three keys together you end up with a charm that increases your luck and helps open symbolic doors that lead to love, health, and prosperity.

RABBIT'S FOOT

A rabbit's foot is a longtime symbol of luck. According to legend, if you catch a rabbit in a cemetery at night and keep its left hind foot, you will be able to ward off evil spirits. Not so lucky for the rabbit.

WISHBONE

Traditionally, this fork-shaped bone is put aside to dry until it is brittle. Once it's ready, two people each hold on to a side of the bone and make a silent wish. They slowly pull the bone apart until it breaks. The person who ends up with the larger piece will have their wish come true. A wishbone necklace is considered a gift of good fortune and an expression of hope that luck will befall the recipient.

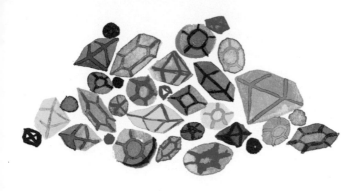

CRYSTALS AND GEMSTONES

Many different stones are considered lucky but their effectiveness can change depending on what stage you are in life. Stones can be combined in different configurations to generate even more luck. Because of this, you'll have to experiment in order to achieve the most luck possible for yourself. Some basic lucky stones include:

AGATE

Brings luck in: Protection
This stone offers safety to the one who holds it.

AMAZONITE

Brings luck in: Hopes and dreams
Also known as the "lucky hope stone," it's thought to
increase the possibility of making all your hopes and
dreams come true by bringing clarity and truth to your
intention.

AVENTURINE

Brings luck in: Winning
Often called the "stone of opportunity," it boosts your
chance of winning, particularly at times when the situation is out of your control. Aventurine doubles your luck
and is thought to be very lucky for those who gamble.

BLOODSTONE

Brings luck in: Endurance
Athletes are thought to get additional endurance and
physical energy.

CARNELIAN

Brings luck in: Confidence
Brings creative energy and courage and dispels fear. It
offers luck for those who make presentations. It's also
good for actors.

CAT'S EYE

Brings luck in: Positivity
Sometimes called the tail of the dragon, it protects the
owner from negative forces. It creates a smooth energy
flow, which is great for removing creative blocks.

CORAL

Brings luck in: Wealth
For those in need of a stable career and success in
business, it is supposed to bring material happiness. It
is often called the "prosperity stone."

HEMATITE

Brings luck in: Relationships
Those who hold this stone will be able to understand
people and improve their relationships.

JASPER

Brings luck in: Serenity
If you are afraid of the dark, the jasper will bring calm.
It's also considered lucky for actors.

MALACHITE

Brings luck in: Business
This stone protects you from unwelcome business
associates and so can be used to bring success in
your career.

ROSE QUARTZ

Brings luck in: Love
For those who want to make way for love and compassion. Rose quartz will help you find love and also add
spice and heat to your current relationship.

SODALITE

Brings luck in: Courage
For peace of mind and getting rid of worries, it
builds confidence in introverts and brings knowledge
and intelligence. Sodalite is a favorite of actors
and performers.

ACTIONS FOR LUCK

CROSSING YOUR FINGERS

As a symbol of good luck, one theory dates back to pre-Christian times when the cross's intersection was believed to be a meeting point of good spirits. The junction could also hold onto wishes until they came true. Originally, the crossing of fingers required two people—one would put their finger perpendicular to another's (the person making the wish) to create a cross as a sign of support for the wisher. Eventually the practice only required one person, who would make the cross using one finger from each hand and make a wish for themselves or others. Over time that evolved to today's version where you cross your index and middle fingers to indicate hope for good luck to follow. Don't cross your fingers behind your back, though! That means you are lying about your wish, which is not auspicious.

GIVING A THUMBS-UP

The thumbs-up is an almost universal symbol of good luck in the English-speaking world. Use it for any situation in which you want someone to do well, from success in sports to wishing someone luck on a job interview. Be careful using this symbol abroad, however, since it has a negative connotation in some countries.

KNOCKING ON WOOD

You can actually knock on wood or just invoke this phrase to preserve luck or avoid tempting fate. Its use could go back as far as pagan times when people thought spirits lived in trees. They would go to a tree, knock on the trunk, and whisper their hopes and dreams. The knocking was supposed to keep evil spirits from hearing what they said.

KNOCKING THREE TIMES

If someone you know is beginning a journey, it's customary to knock three times on the door with your knuckles to wish them a safe journey.

LEAVING THINGS BEHIND

It's unlucky to forget something and go back for it. But don't wait too long, because the longer it takes to get back to retrieve the object, the more bad luck will accumulate.

LOOKING OVER YOUR RIGHT SHOULDER

Some stories say that an angel sits on your right shoulder and a devil on your left. So harness yourself some good luck by looking over your right shoulder instead of your left, which will earn you the opposite.

SWEEPING WITH A NEW BROOM

If you have a new broom, use it to sweep something into your home before you sweep out any dirt or you run the risk of sweeping out all your good luck.

THROWING SALT OVER YOUR SHOULDER

If you spill some salt (a sign of bad luck), you can try to turn your luck around by taking a pinch of it and throwing it over your left shoulder, which will blind the devil who is believed to always wait there.

WISHING ON A STAR

Early Europeans believed that the gods, while moving the sky from day to night, would occasionally look down at the mortals below and get a bit careless and drop a star. In Greek culture it was thought that the stars were actually human souls. Either way, it was considered lucky to make a wish when you saw one. Wish upon a star if you're in need of a little bit of magic and some positive vibes.

AUSPICIOUS DAYS

SUNDAY

This is often considered the luckiest day to be born, and those born on this day are considered protected from witches or evil spirits. Medicines or any attempts to heal on this day are more likely to succeed. In some parts of the United Kingdom and United States, people avoid sealing agreements on Sundays to avoid offending God. If you want to maintain good luck on a Sunday, don't change your sheets or cut your nails. Sewing and darning is also not to be done on a Sunday—it was thought that the devil would thread the needle. And if you're going on a journey, start on a Sunday for the best luck.

MONDAY

Due to Monday's connection with the moon, it is linked to women and emotions. Any emotions will be stronger, so make sure they are good ones. Monday is also a good day to move.

TUESDAY

Some say to meet a left-handed person early on a Tuesday morning will bring much bad luck for the rest of the day. Tuesday is a great day for trying new things at work; it is a day of improvement, growth, and promotion.

WEDNESDAY

In most of Europe, Wednesday is not an auspicious day, but the Persians called Wednesday the "red letter" day, which was good, probably because they believed the moon was created on this day. Wednesday is a day of creativity, so give in to your artistic nature today. Your communication skills will improve on a Wednesday too; aim to follow up on that call or email on this day.

THURSDAY

Consider your finances on a Thursday. Change an existing or plan a new budget on this day. Or reexamine any money goals you may have. If you live in Germany, wait for another day. This is considered the most unlucky day of the week, so much so that at one time, no business was done on Thursday, no one got married, and even kids could not go to school if it was their first day.

FRIDAY

Unfortunately, in many Christian countries, Friday is considered unlucky, mostly because Jesus was believed to have died on this day. Some say too that it's the day Eve was tempted by the serpent. Things to avoid on Fridays: births, weddings, starting a new job, embarking on a voyage, or cutting your nails. In Scottish and German history, the belief was that Friday was a lucky day for courting. Things to do on a Friday: go to a party, hang out with friends, enjoy a date.

SATURDAY

In India, this is considered an unlucky day because of its association with Shani, the god of misfortune. In Irish lore, if a rainbow appears on a Saturday it will rain for the entire following week. Children born on a Saturday in Scotland are thought to be able to see ghosts. And in the United Kingdom, it's bad luck to change jobs on a Saturday based on an old rhyme, "Saturday servants never stay, Sunday servants run away." Spend your Saturdays relaxing and generating positivity.

There's also a little poem about luck related to the day you were born:

> Monday's child is fair of face;
> Tuesday's child is full of grace;
> Wednesday's child is full of woe;
> Thursday's child has far to go;
> Friday's child is loving and giving;
> Saturday's child works hard for its living;
> But the child born on the Sabbath is blithe
> and bonny and good and gay.

AUSPICIOUS NUMBERS

In general, odd numbers are considered luckier than even numbers, and references to the auspiciousness of odd numbers has been mentioned in the writings of Virgil and Plutarch. Chinese pagodas (sacred towers) always have an odd number of stories and are built to increase the luck of a neighborhood. In ancient Thailand, all houses had to have an uneven number of rooms, windows, and doors, and an odd number of stairs.

ONE

One is symbolic of beginnings and new starts, which makes it auspicious. It is also seen as a number of achievement.

TWO

Ancient Egyptians believed this number represented knowledge and wisdom. If you had both of these you were considered very lucky. Two is also associated with harmonious partnerships.

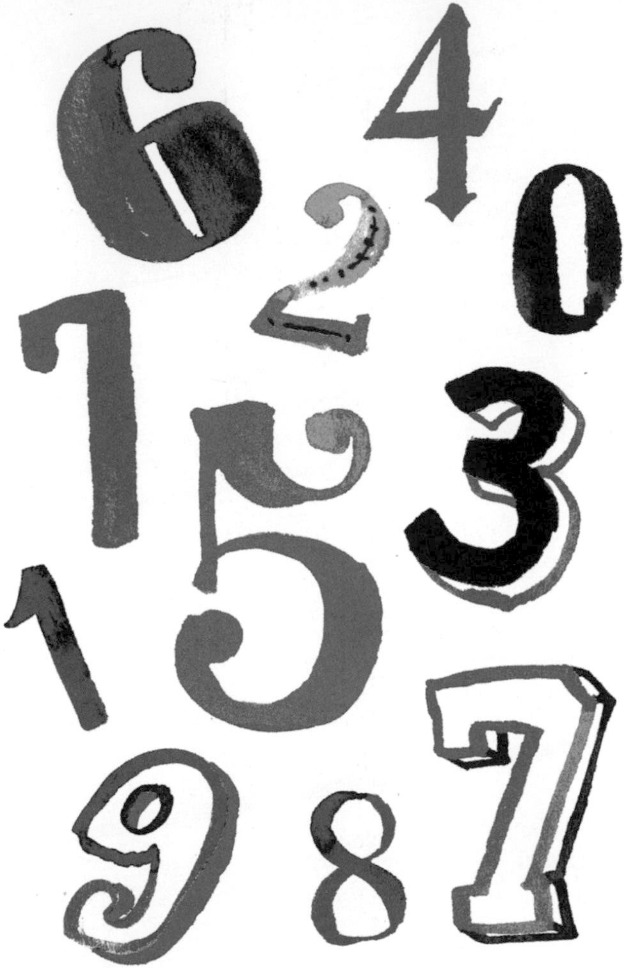
6 4
2 0
1 5 3
1
9 8 7

THREE

The number three is considered lucky in practically every ancient culture and religion. Mythology is full of threes: Neptune's trident, the Three Graces, Cerberus the three-headed dog. Hindu culture reveres threes, and three is sacred in Judaism, Christianity, and pagan religions from Western Europe.

FOUR

This is a lucky number if you are in need of protection or are focusing on the home. It is associated with Horus, the Egyptian god of war and hunting, who was the son of Isis and Osiris. In Chinese culture though, the number four sounds very close to the word for death in Mandarin and is considered very unlucky.

FIVE

In China, this number is connected to five blessings: health, wealth, life, peace, and luck. It is thought to be a lucky number for physical health and protection. In the Bible, David threw five stones at Goliath before defeating him.

SIX

If you are looking for love or a new relationship, six is your lucky number. That is the number on the Lovers card in the tarot and is also connected to Venus, who inspires passion.

SEVEN

This number is lucky in many cultures and countries. The Greeks saw it as a perfect number (three, representing a triangle, plus four, representing a square—both are considered perfect forms). Seven is a number that has completely infiltrated our daily lives: seven days of the week; seven colors of the rainbow; seven notes on a scale; seven seas; and seven planets can be seen with the naked eye. Seven can't be divided by half so people who like this number are those who see themselves as individuals—more appealing than the average person. If you are the seventh son of a seventh son you are supposed to be extremely lucky. The number seven is auspicious for academic and spiritual achievement.

EIGHT

In Chinese culture, eight is a symbol of infinity and very auspicious. When turned on its side, the number eight becomes an infinity symbol and implies that what is lost will eventually be found. Its cyclical nature gives hope that good luck will return after bad times. It embodies balance and harmony, both of which help ensure increased luck.

NINE

This is lucky because of its association with the number three. It's a great number to focus on when trying to combine inspiration from many sources into one cohesive statement.

THIRTEEN

Pretty much always considered an unlucky number, it even spawned its own technical word to describe it—triskaidekaphobia, fear of the number thirteen. In Mayan culture, the thirteenth *baktun* (cycle) marks the end of their calendar and is said to be the time of the apocalypse. In Tarot, thirteen is the card of death. Friday the thirteenth is considered very unlucky—approximately seventeen million people are afraid of this day.

LUCKY SAYINGS

Most sayings about luck imply that good fortune comes to those who work hard to improve their fate, which you can see from the common proverbs below.

* Find a penny, pick it up, all the day you'll have good luck.

* A lucky man always ends as a fool.

* A stout man crushes good luck. (Spanish)

* Everyone is the author of his own good luck. (Italian)

- Bad luck comes in pounds and goes away by ounces. (Italian)

- An ounce of good luck is better than a ton of brains.

- Against a lucky man, even a god has little power. (Latin)

- Luck is always borrowed, never owned. (Norwegian)

- It is better that the luck seek the man than the man seek the luck. (Yiddish)

- Bad luck comes in threes.

- Luck does not favor wisdom. (Roman)

- Better an ounce of luck than a pound of gold. (Yiddish)

❖ Luck is when opportunity knocks and you answer.

❖ Luck never gives, it only lends. (Swedish)

❖ For each petal on the shamrock, this brings a wish your way. Good health, good luck, and happiness for today and every day. (Irish)

❖ Good luck comes in slender currents, misfortune in a rolling tide. (Irish)

QUOTES ABOUT LUCK

"Diligence is the mother of good luck."
—*Benjamin Franklin*

"I am a great believer in luck. The harder I work, the more of it I seem to have."
—*Coleman Cox*

"Each misfortune you encounter will carry in it the seed of tomorrow's good luck."
—*Og Mandino*

"Luck is a dividend of sweat. The more you sweat, the luckier you will get."
—*Ray A. Kroc*

"The only sure thing about luck is that it will change."
—*Bret Harte*

"Luck is what happens when preparation
meets opportunity."

—*Seneca*

"Luck is not something you can mention in the presence
of self-made men."

—*E. B. White*

"Nothing is as obnoxious as other people's luck."

—*F. Scott Fitzgerald*

"The best luck of all is the luck you make for yourself."

—*Douglas MacArthur*

"When it comes to luck, you make your own."

—*Bruce Springsteen*

"A pound of pluck is worth a ton of luck."

—*James A. Garfield*

"Luck affects everything. Let your hook always be cast; in the stream where you least expect it there will be a fish."

—*Ovid*

"I think we consider too much the good luck of the early bird and not enough the bad luck of the early worm."

—*Franklin D. Roosevelt*

10 MOVIES ABOUT LUCK

1. *Lucky You* (2007)

2. *Lucky Numbers* (2000)

3. *Lucky* (2011)

4. *Good Night and Good Luck* (2005)

5. *Just My Luck* (2006)

6. *Lucky Luke* (2009)

7. *Logan Lucky* (2017)

8. *The Lucky Ones* (2008)

9. *The Luck of the Irish* (1948)

10. *The Joy Luck Club* (1993)

10 SONGS ABOUT LUCK

1. "Some Guys Have all the Luck,"
written by Jeff Fortgang, originally
recorded by The Persuaders. 1974

2. "With a Little Luck,"
by Paul McCartney and Wings. 1978

3. "Lucky Star,"
by Madonna. 1983

4. "Superstition,"
by Stevie Wonder. 1972

5. "A Good Run of Bad Luck,"
by Clint Black. 1993

6. "Just Got Lucky,"
by JoBoxers. 1983

7. "Lucky to Be Me,"
by Bill Evans. 1959

8. "Bad Luck,"
   by Harold Melvin and the Blue Notes.
   1975

9. "Get Lucky,"
   by Daft Punk. 2013

10. "Luck Be a Lady,"
    written by Frank Loesser, made
    famous by Frank Sinatra. 1950

CHAPTER 3

LUCKY YOU

BIRTHSTONES

JANUARY

Garnet—Represents peace, prosperity, and good health. Some say it can give eternal happiness to the person who wears it. It also encourages good business relationships.

FEBRUARY

Amethyst—A symbol of peace, courage, and stability. Its psychic power can make your dreams come true.

MARCH

Aquamarine—Promotes confidence and creativity. Also preserves and enhances the health of the one who wears it.

APRIL

Diamond—Bestows luck, prosperity, and faithfulness.

MAY

Emerald—Embodies unconditional love, unity, and compassion; it is sometimes called "the stone of successful love."

JUNE

Pearl—Symbolizes affection and pure love. Also considered good luck.

JULY

Ruby—A talisman of prosperity and passion, it is often worn to protect oneself from plague or other negative situations. It will bring the wearer peace.

AUGUST

Peridot—Increases willpower, growth, and optimism. It is said to help achieve goals after the release of any negativity. Also helps with making dreams come true.

SEPTEMBER

Sapphire—Brings good fortune and spiritual insight. If worn as an amulet, it protects from poison, plague, or fever and resists all forms of black magic.

OCTOBER

Tourmaline—Comes in many colors and each is auspicious in its own way. Green tourmaline brings wholesome energy to the body and is thought to heal. The pink version encourages compassion and gentleness. Red is all about love and is great for revitalizing passion. It also brings one a zest for life.

NOVEMBER

Topaz/Citrine—Grants true love, fidelity, and friendship. Sometimes called the "merchant's stone" because it ensures luck in business, self-assurance, confidence, and prosperity. Dispels negative energy.

DECEMBER

Turquoise—Brings harmony. It is the gem to wear if you want to find yourself and achieve serenity.

PARTS OF THE BODY

BELLY BUTTON

If a woman has a deep navel, she will live a long and happy life.

CHIN

If a man has little or no hair on his chin, he will be bad with money, selfish, and cowardly.

EYEBROWS

Eyebrows with scant hair are considered unlucky.

EYES

If your eyes are red in the corners, that's lucky.

FEET

If there are spiral marks on the soles of your feet, good fortune will follow and your struggles will be few. But If your toes are longer than typical, that is not auspicious and you will suffer in life.

HAIR

Red hair is auspicious. A sudden loss of hair is unlucky and will lead to a decline in health. Cutting your hair on a Friday is very bad luck, and if you cut your own hair, you are tempting fate (probably beyond just superstition if you have no hairdressing skills!).

HANDS

If a woman's thumb is wide and round she will be surrounded by good luck.

MOLES

There are many lucky signs and superstitions associated with moles depending on where they are on your body. The size and shape is also a determining factor in whether a mole is good or bad luck:

❖ Women with a mole or wart below their belly button are considered lucky and will have prosperity and happiness in their lives.

❖ Wealth is also said to come to women with a mole on their nose.

❖ If a mole is on the left side of your forehead or nose, this is unlucky and you will be selfish.

❖ In Chinese culture, it's better to have a mole on the front of your body. A mole on your back indicates that there may be a struggle ahead. However, in

English culture, "a mole on the back, money by the sack."

- ❖ A man with a mole near his armpit will have luck in finances. For a woman, the mole must be between the elbow and wrist to achieve financial freedom.

- ❖ A mole on the back of a thigh is always good luck for both men and women.

NOSE

If you have a nose like a parrot's beak, you will have wonderful luck and are likely to rule.

TEETH

You will have luck with finances if you have long teeth. It's auspicious to have a large gap in your teeth.

TONGUE

A soft pink tongue brings good fortune in the form of happiness for you and your entire family.

COLORS

Many colors are supposed to bring good luck, and much superstition is attached to wearing certain colors at certain times to generate positive energy and scare away evil.

BLACK

Most often associated with darkness, the unknown, death, grief, or hate, the color black is also related to dignity. It is considered a lucky color if you were born under the signs of Libra, Aquarius, or Capricorn.

BLUE

This has been a sacred color dating back to ancient times; it is still sacred today due to its association with the Virgin Mary. In parts of Europe, many women believe the color protects babies from fevers so they often wear a blue neckband when breastfeeding. Blue represents truth, honesty, tranquility, and openness. Aquarius, Libra, and Taurus will find luck with blue.

BROWN

Only the paler hues of brown are considered lucky, and if your sign is Cancer, it's best to avoid it entirely. It is, however, a symbol of the earth and has positive attributes like practicality and physical comfort.

BURGUNDY OR DEEP WINE RED

This is a symbol of power, wealth, and prosperity.

GOLD

A color associated with the sun is lucky for pretty much everyone. Wear it to find refinement and spiritual rewards.

GREEN

Green functions as a lucky color for some, particularly if you were born under the sign of Capricorn or Aquarius. The color indicates that you could experience a positive change, good health, growth, and healing. However, if you're an actor, beware! In theater, this color is very unlucky. This superstition goes back to the time when the stage was lit with lights that burned lime (the origin of limelight) and produced light with a green tinge to it. If you wore green clothing, the light would make you look almost invisible—the exact opposite of the goals of the actor.

ORANGE

A great color for those seeking warmth, happiness, intelligence, youthfulness, and motivation.

PINK

This hue symbolizes devotion and romance. A great color to promote affection, love, joy, sweetness, and kindness.

PURPLE

In ancient times, the color purple was extremely rare and therefore expensive, which is why it's mostly associated with royalty. If you are a Pisces or Sagittarius, purple is a very lucky color and will bring you creativity, passion, healing ability, kindness, and compassion.

RED

Lucky for Aries and Scorpio, but avoid red if you are a Libra or Taurus. In China and other Asian countries, red is by far the most auspicious color. It symbolizes power, passion, energy, love, and life.

SILVER

Embodies justice and purity.

TURQUOISE

Some say turquoise has a great deal of healing power and spiritual energy. It is connected to the sun and fire.

WHITE

Although considered lucky for those born under Cancer, Gemini, or Virgo, white can be very unlucky in some cultures where white is the color of death and mourning. But elsewhere it is considered a sign of innocence and purity, peace, and dignity.

YELLOW

Like gold, yellow is closely connected to the sun, and therefore is lucky for many people. Leos can bask in its sunny glory, but a Virgo or Taurus should stay away from it. Yellow is a symbol of hope, optimism, joy, cheer, and increased energy.

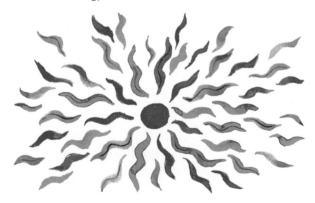

NAMES

There are some names whose meanings relate to luck. Any one of these could be an auspicious choice if you find yourself choosing names.

GIRLS

DALIA
(Lithuanian) luck, fate

DESTINY
(French) fate

EVANGELINE
(Greek) bringer of good news

FAUSTINA
(Latin) fortunate one

FELICIA
(Latin) lucky, fortunate (var. Felicity)

HALONA
(Native American, tribe unknown) happy fortune

KALYANI
(Hindu) beautiful, auspicious

LAKSHMI
(Hindu) a good omen

MACHIKO
(Japanese) fortunate child

MOIRA
(Greek) destiny

SADIYA
(Arabic) (var. Zadia) lucky, fortunate

SHREYA
(Hindu) lucky

BOYS

ASHER
(Hebrew) blessed one

CHANCE
(English) luck, fortune

EDMUND
(English) fortunate protector

FAUST
(Greek) (var. Fausto) fortunate

FELIX
(Latin) fortunate one

JUN-SEO
(Korean) good omen, auspicious, talented

MADOC
(Welsh) fortunate (var. Maddox)

PARVAIZ
(Persian) lucky, happy

SA'ID
(Arabic) happy, lucky (var. Saad, Sadah)

VENTURO
(Spanish) good luck

YOSHI
(Japanese) good luck, virtuous, respectable
(var. Hideyoshi)

AND A FEW NAMES WHOSE VERY MEANING IS MISFORTUNE OR SADNESS:

BRONA
(Irish) sadness, sorrow

DESDEMONA
(Greek) ill-fated

DOLORES
(Spanish) sorrow (var. Lola, Lolita)

JABEZ
(Hebrew) sorrow

MALLORY
(French) ill-fated luck, unfortunate

NEKANE
(Basque) sorrows

CLOTHING

It has been said that "clothes make the man," but clothes and how you wear them also make good luck—and bad.

BELTS

Some think that belts, which wrap around your body, offer protection from sorcerers. But be careful about throwing away a belt because if a witch finds it, your luck will fade away.

BUTTONS

An odd number of buttons on an item of clothing is auspicious. If you count an even number, never fear, just sew on another button to get the desired positive effect. Finding a button is also lucky and if you do, keep it in your pocket as a talisman. And if you are one of those people that keeps a container of buttons, even better, because that's considered lucky too.

GLOVES

If you drop a glove, it's unlucky to pick it up yourself. Wait and let someone else pick it up for you, which is auspicious. (Who knows? Perhaps you'll meet the love of your life!)

HANDKERCHIEFS

Tie a knot in your handkerchief to scare away evil by distracting the devil. He'll be so intrigued by it, he will leave you alone.

HATS

It's bad luck to put on a hat back to front—you will have a very bad day.

POLKA DOTS

These are thought to look like an abundance of coins, so legend has it that polka dots on clothing will bring prosperity into your life.

SHOES

Make a wish while tying someone else's shoelaces—it's considered lucky. Putting your right shoe on first is lucky too.

SOCKS

It's lucky to discover you have a hole in your sock but don't wear that same sock the next day unless you fix the hole or it's bad luck.

SOMETHING BLUE

When in doubt, wear something blue, the color of the sky and the heavens. This will bring you success.

HOW TO TREAT YOUR CLOTHES:

Giving Away Your Old Clothes. Giving your clothes to someone sick or very old is very unlucky.

Putting a Coin in a Pocket. Coins are already lucky for a number of reasons (see page 45) but if you put one in the pocket of a new pair of pants or a new shirt before you wear it for the first time, good things should come your way. Whatever coin you use, don't ever spend it if you want to be sure to retain the luck.

Wearing Your Clothes Inside Out. If you accidentally wear a piece of clothing inside out, that's considered lucky (this applies to socks too) and if you suddenly notice you've done this or if someone points it out, don't correct the error. Continue to wear the item inside out to receive the full benefit of the magic.

IN THE KITCHEN

❖ When mixing up ingredients, always be sure to stir clockwise. This belief goes back to when people worshipped the sun and thought it was lucky to do everything from east to west.

❖ When baking bread, mark your loaves with a cross to ward off evil spirits.

❖ Salt can be both lucky and unlucky (see Actions for Luck, page 58), but the ancient Greeks believed it was sacred, probably because salt was a preservative and helped to ensure a supply of food for the year. It is often given to babies as a gift of good luck. Traders would carry a small bag of salt in their pocket to bring them good luck in their business dealings.

❖ An apron that suddenly falls off is bad luck.

❖ If you are washing the dishes and break one, you will break something else before the end of the day. To counter this, quickly break another dish and that will dispel the bad luck (unfortunately, you get two broken dishes).

❖ Change your seat at the table and risk a run of bad luck. An engaged woman should never sit on a table while talking to her fiancé—it will bring much bad luck.

CHAPTER 4

LUCKY IN LOVE

FINDING LOVE

Finding love has always felt like a mixture of luck and fate. Here are some things you can do to increase your chances of finding and keeping love in your life.

BUBBLES

Finding bubbles in a noncarbonated drink foretells luck in love.

CATS

There is much ado about cats and luck generally, but crossing the path of a tortoiseshell cat is good luck if you are seeking love.

EYELASHES

Wish on an eyelash that has fallen to have luck finding your true love.

FLOWERS

If you want to show feelings of love for someone by giving them a gift, be sure to avoid yellow flowers—these signify the end of a relationship and are considered unlucky for new couples.

FOUR-LEAF CLOVERS

Four-leaf clovers are thought to bring much good fortune in love. If you put one in your shoe, your spouse will have the same first name as the man or woman you see right after you place it there.

KNOTS

Knots are a symbol of love and connection, and finding one is a fortuitous omen for your love life. But don't undo the knot, lest you undo the luck as well.

SITTING

Be careful where you sit at the table. Sitting near the corner of a table, or even worse, on the table, will lead to an unlucky love life.

STAIRS

If you stumble while going up the stairs, don't sweat it. It's a sign that love will soon come your way.

STEPPING ON TOES

Stepping on your loved one's foot by accident will bring disharmony into your relationship, but you can counteract that by having them lightly step on your foot in return.

GETTING MARRIED

GETTING READY

CHOOSING THE DATE

Deciding on when to get married can be as fraught as choosing to get married at all. To help ease the process, here's some advice on the most auspicious days for a wedding:

JANUARY
2, 16, 25

FEBRUARY
6, 18, 29

MARCH
14, 15, 21

APRIL
2, 3, 24

MAY

7, 21, 24

JUNE

4, 12, 24

JULY

9, 17, 30

AUGUST

6, 20, 21

SEPTEMBER

10, 18, 19

OCTOBER

7, 9, 15

NOVEMBER

5, 20, 27

DECEMBER

4, 10, 31

When it comes to the day of the week, Wednesday is the most auspicious day for a wedding while Saturday is considered the unluckiest. An old poem sums it up—

"Monday for health
Tuesday for wealth
Wednesday best of all
Thursday for losses
Friday for crosses
Saturday for no luck at all."

COINS

It's traditional in Sweden for the mother and father of the bride to give a gold coin and a silver coin, respectively, to the bride, who would put one in each shoe to make sure the couple would never want for anything in their marriage. Other similar traditions call for a "silver sixpence in her shoe," which is given as a token to wish the bride happiness in her new life. As far back as the reign of Elizabeth I, it was the lord of the manor where the bride lived who would provide the sixpence. Over time, the giver has changed, and it's sometimes the groom or the father of the bride who presents the sixpence.

Regardless, once the sixpence is in the shoe, the bride is to walk in a circle while making a wish for future wealth.

DRESS

In Asian countries, the dress might be embroidered with cranes, which will ensure a long and happy marriage. Red is also a lucky color for brides in China, India, Pakistan, and Vietnam. In Japan, the dress has always been traditionally white, though in the Western world white wedding dresses didn't become popular until Queen Victoria wore a white dress at her own wedding in 1840. However, in countries like Korea, bright colors are considered auspicious for the wedding dress. In Denmark, couples would try to confuse evil spirits or goblins by swapping clothes.

The one color for a bride to avoid in her wedding clothes is black. Not only is it believed to lead to an unhappy marriage, like in the old rhyme "Married in black, you'll wish yourself back," but it is also believed to lead to the untimely death of one of the newlyweds, since widows wear black.

SIXPENCE

The oft forgotten last line of the "something old" ditty is "and a sixpence in her shoe." A sixpence piece, placed in the bride's left shoe, will bring good fortune and prosperity to the couple. If you can't find a real sixpence, an old coin from the country of the bride's ancestors will do just fine.

SOMETHING OLD, SOMETHING NEW, SOMETHING BORROWED, SOMETHING BLUE

This is a popular tradition for brides to follow on their wedding day. *Something old* represents the bride's past and childhood. *Something new* looks forward to her future as a married woman. *Something borrowed* is an offering from a friend or family member who is already happily married and will give good luck to the new married couple. *Something blue* is a symbol of love and eternal fidelity.

SPIDERS

In many cultures, finding a spider or other eight-legged insect on the wedding dress is considered a lucky omen. Really, don't panic.

SUGAR

Your married life will be even sweeter if you put a sugar cube in your glove or somewhere in your gown.

TIMING

No matter what hour of the day or night you get married, the most auspicious time to say your vows is at the top of the hour while the minute hand is pointing up.

VEILS

In ancient Greek and Roman culture, the bride would wear a veil that completely covered her as she walked to protect her from evil spirits who would try to destroy her happiness.

THE CEREMONY

BOUQUETS

Orange blossoms are considered the most traditional wedding flower and a sign of the couple's everlasting love for each other. A sprig of ivy is often part of a bouquet and is associated with fidelity and happiness for the newly wedded couple. For additional luck, the ivy could be planted with the intention of passing on the couple's happiness to their children and grandchildren. It's common in brides of Irish descent to put bells in their bouquets to scare away evil spirits. They also add lavender to the bouquet for happiness.

CRYING

It's natural for the bride to cry on her wedding day, but it's good luck too. It symbolizes that those tears are the last she will ever shed, because her new life will be wonderful.

GIVING AWAY THE BRIDE

Originally, this was done because, as the property of her father, the bride had to be given to the groom—often for a price. As time went by, customs changed and this tradition has become more symbolic of the blessing and wishes for good luck that her father bestows on the new couple.

THE RINGS

The wedding and engagement rings are traditionally worn on the fourth finger of the left hand. It was generally thought that a vein in that finger leads directly to the heart, so it was a sign of good luck. For future marital happiness, a sapphire or an aquamarine should be part

of the ring. But no pearls in the engagement ring—it's a symbol of tears and an unhappy marriage.

THE RECEPTION

Bread: Couples in Romania share bread, traditionally shaped in a braid and baked by the godmother. It's said that if you eat a piece, you will have good luck all year long.

BREAKING GLASS

If you think breaking glass is bad luck, think again. In Italy, it's traditional for the groom to smash a glass or a vase into as many pieces as possible—the more pieces, the longer the marriage will last. And in Germany, if you smash a few dishes the night before you get married, nothing in your new life will ever get broken again. Breaking a glass is also part of the Jewish wedding ceremony, and it's traditional to say *Mazal Tov*, meaning good luck, when the glass is broken.

THE CAKE

This tradition started in ancient Rome when guests would break a loaf of bread over the bride's head to wish the couple luck in having children. Over time it changed into a cake and the luck was in cutting the cake. The cake-topper tradition was started by Queen Victoria and has come to be a symbol of good luck and stability in the marriage. It is unlucky for a bride to make her own cake.

DECORATIONS

Koreans put a pair of ducks near where the couple says their vows, which implies a life of togetherness. In England, carrying a horseshoe decorated in ribbons during the ceremony foretells a blissful life for the couple. In Cambodia, if you bring a sword to the wedding it's a sign of harmony and strength and will make the couple's wishes come true. Flowers are almost always welcome at weddings and are generally considered to encourage fertility, represent purity, and chase away any lurking evil spirits.

FAVORS

Having wooden spoons as wedding favors encourages productivity in the kitchen. In Scotland, instead of a spoon, they'll often use a spirtle, a special wooden stick made for stirring porridge. At weddings in Thailand, guests are each given white strings called *sai sin* to wrap around the couple's wrists for luck. To intensify that luck, the couple wears them for three days.

PINCHING

In Egypt, some brides would get a pinch for luck on their wedding day from the female guests.

TOSSING THE BOUQUET

This tradition may come from a time when female guests would try to tear off actual pieces of the bride's dress or parts of her bouquet in an effort to gather some of the bride's luck for themselves. The bride would avoid this by throwing the bouquet, which would distract the women and give the couple a few seconds to run away. The tossing of the bouquet is still a tradition at most weddings, and the bride often throws it backward over her shoulder, and the single woman who catches it will be the next lucky bride.

MISCELLANEOUS

AVOIDING EACH OTHER BEFORE THE WEDDING

Back when marriages were arranged, the bride and groom were discouraged from seeing each other before the ceremony to avoid any second thoughts one or the other might have.

CHOOSING A DAY

Modern weddings are generally on Saturdays or Sundays, but English tradition says the worst day to marry is Saturday and the best day to marry is actually Wednesday. Regarding the perfect month to be married, June seems to be the big winner because it is named after Juno, the goddess of marriage and family, which makes that month luckier than others.

RAIN

If it rains on your wedding day, it's actually a sign of good luck for the new husband and wife because it symbolizes fertility and cleansing. But in the American South, a bottle of bourbon is buried upside down right where the ceremony will be performed at least a month in advance to prevent rain on the wedding day. After the couple is married, it can be dug up and savored.

SCARING OFF THE EVIL EYE

For traditional Jewish ceremonies, the bride will circle around the groom three or seven times while they are under the chuppah. This is thought to protect the couple from evil spirits or any temptations from other women. In the Middle East, the hands and feet of the bride are decorated with henna to scare off the evil eye. The darker the henna, the more good luck will be accumulated. After the ceremony, in China, fireworks are lit to scare away any evil spirits.

STARTING AN AUSPICIOUS LIFE TOGETHER

COINS

In Poland, guests throw coins over the bride and groom, and it's auspicious for the couple to gather the coins themselves as their first task together as a married couple. And after the ceremony, it's traditional to pay the wedding officiant in an odd amount of money, which is considered lucky for the couple.

PLANTS

In the Netherlands, it's customary to plant lilies of the valley at the couple's home to ensure that their love will be renewed every year. And planting pine trees is also customary to bring good luck in fertility.

RICE OR CONFETTI

It's traditional to throw rice, confetti, flowers, grains, almonds, and more at the departing couple as they leave the reception. Long ago, this was a symbolic wish to the couple for fertility and is still a frequent part of weddings, though today it's more for good wishes than a houseful of children. In the Czech Republic, guests throw peas instead of rice to wish luck to the happy couple, but the idea remains the same.

THE THRESHOLD

In medieval times, many people thought a bride was at risk of attracting evil spirits through the soles of her feet. The groom would carry her over the threshold to protect his new wife and keep those spirits away from their home. Carrying the bride also avoided another aspect of bad luck—the bride tripping or falling as she walks into her new home. In Nigeria, newly married couples wash their feet with cold water before walking over the threshold for the first time in their new home. Based on Yoruba tradition, this will ensure that the couple starts their new life with no worries.

BAD LUCK FOR WEDDINGS

* Some think that it's bad luck if the bride and groom have the same first letter in their last name.

* It's very bad luck to buy the engagement and wedding rings at the same time. And one should never wear the wedding ring before the actual ceremony either.

* An engaged woman should never write her married name before the ceremony. In fact, years ago, wedding linen was often embroidered with the bride's maiden initials to avoid bad luck.

* Wearing the wedding dress before the wedding will bring such bad luck that many brides will make sure that the dress is incomplete right up to the last fitting. In some cultures, it's traditional for the last stitch of a wedding dress to be sewn as the bride is traveling to the church on her wedding day.

* Giving a knife as a gift is considered unlucky because it symbolizes a break or separation of the relationship. The couple can counteract this by offering the gift giver one penny, which means they have now paid for the knife and it's no longer a gift.

❖ Don't wear pearls on the day of the wedding. It represents tears and unhappiness.

❖ It's bad luck if the younger of two sisters marries first, but it can be counteracted if the older sister dances barefoot at her sister's wedding.

❖ If the bridal party passes a hearse on the way to the wedding, it's very bad luck.

❖ The marriage will never last if the groom drops the wedding ring during the ceremony.

❖ Candles that are lit and then sputter out on the wedding day are thought to indicate that evil spirits are close by and may threaten the couple.

CHAPTER 5

LUCK AROUND THE WORLD

ARGENTINA

Beans. If you eat beans on New Year's Eve or New Year's Day in Argentina, you will have luck and job security for the coming year.

Grapes. A common New Year's Eve tradition is to eat twelve grapes right at midnight. If you can eat them within twelve seconds you will have a year of good fortune.

AUSTRALIA

Arsey. This refers to someone experiencing very good luck in a near-miss situation.

Chookas. This is an Australian word used to wish those in the theater good luck—much like "break a leg."

Frogs. Frogs bring thunder and rain.

Seahorses. The Torres Strait Islanders of Queensland believe the seahorse is a sign of good fortune and a symbol of strength and power. It's used whenever anyone is in need of food.

BOLIVIA

Ekeko. This is the god of prosperity, abundance, and good fortune in Bolivia and Peru. As a talisman or charm, Ekeko is in the shape of a man with a moustache who wears traditional clothing. The owner attaches small items to him as an offering—teeny packages of food, toy cars, even money—to represent what is wished for. However, as an unselfish gesture, the god should then be given to someone the owner truly wants good things for. An interesting side tradition has one put a lit cigarette in Ekeko's mouth. The longer it stays lit, the more likely your wishes will come true. Only one Ekeko should be in a home—if you keep more than one, they will fight with each other and ignore your wishes.

Underwear. In Bolivia, white, yellow, or red underwear is lucky. Black underwear is unlucky and considered the same as walking under a ladder.

BRAZIL

Figa. The Figa charm is popular in Brazil and is represented as a clenched fist with index finder held over the thumb. This is a protective charm that wards off bad energy and brings the bearer good fortune. Some say it holds all the luck that you have yet to use.

CHILE

Money. On New Year's Eve, it's customary to put money in shoes to ensure good luck during the upcoming year.

CHINA

Chinese Guardian Lions. Sometimes known as Foo Dogs, Fu Dogs, or even Buddha Dogs, the Chinese are more likely to call them *shi* because it means "lion." The Japanese call them *komainu*. Whatever they are called, these statues of lions are placed inside or outside of the home or office and will protect the building and everything in it from evil spirits. The guardian lions have been a symbol of luck since the Han dynasty, and several pairs of guardian lions can be found in the Forbidden City in Beijing.

Pixiu. Pixiu is a symbol of luck and has the head of a dragon, a body like a horse, a horn like a deer, and the claws of a lion. It sometimes has wings. It is thought to bring much wealth into the home or office, and as long as Pixiu is in place, the wealth will not leave. Since it attracts money, it's very popular with businessmen, gamblers, and investors. A strange fact about Pixiu is that it does not have an anus—whatever goes in will never come out.

Sweeping. In China, it is believed that good fortune comes in through the front door. Because of this, as people prepare for the New Year, they will be careful to sweep up dirt and dust into a pile away from the front door to avoid losing the luck they already have. It is then disposed of through the back door only.

DENMARK

Broken Dishes. In Denmark, residents save their broken dishes all year, and on New Year's Eve they will throw them at their friends' or neighbors' houses to wish them good luck in the new year. Children will sometimes simply leave a pile of broken dishes on a front step as an alternative to throwing.

Planting a Tree. If newlyweds plant a pine tree outside of their new home, it is supposed to bring good luck and fertility.

EGYPT

Ladders. Ancient Egyptians put ladders in their graves to make sure the dead could get to heaven. Today, the ladder has turned into a sign of good luck.

ETHIOPIA

Buda. Also known as *bouda*, this is an Ethiopian belief in the evil eye, which they believe can change the bearer into a hyena. Ethiopian residents will sometimes carry a *kitab* (talisman), which is supposed to protect them

against any evil curses brought by buda. It's traditionally thought that buda is rooted in jealousy. Other African countries with these beliefs include Sudan, Tanzania, and the Berber people of Morocco.

FINLAND

Tursaansydan (or *mursundsydan*). The "heart of a walrus" was a common symbol of luck in northern Europe, most particularly to those from the most northern region of Finland, called Lapland, where it was often seen on the drums of shamans. Its four interconnected squares depict a swastika, which is an ancient sacred symbol far predating its use by the Nazis, which gave it negative connotations. Originally the heart of the walrus would protect one from curses.

GHANA

Adinkra. These are visual symbols created by the Gyaman in the Ivory Coast and the Ashanti in Ghana. They are often seen as decorative, but many have specific meanings and are held or worn as talismans of good luck.

Diwali Lamps. Used most often during the Diwali festival—the festival of lights. Hindus also use them to worship. Lakshmi is the goddess of wealth, and during the festival of lights everyone seeks to be blessed by her. Lakshmi will not come to a darkened home, and that's where the Diwali lamp comes in; it lights up the house and welcomes her in. This oil-fueled lamp also rids the home of bad energy and ignorance.

Eight Symbols of Good Luck. These symbols of good luck are seen mostly in India, though many other Asian countries, particularly Tibet and China, hold these dear as well. Related to the Buddhist faith, they first appeared on royal insignias but are becoming more popular with the public and, as iconic good luck charms, can be worn as jewelry or displayed in homes. In China and Tibet, the eight auspicious objects represent the body of Buddha, though different countries and cultures disagree on which parts of the body each symbol represents.

❖ **The Banner of Victory**—The banner is thought to help the bearer triumph over the four illusions (the Maras in Tibetan culture) of emotional corruption, lust, passion, and fear of death.

- **The Double Golden Fish**—This has its origin in the Ganges and the Yamuna, two of India's sacred rivers. They bring happiness and life, and encourage fertility and abundance. A pair of fish given as a wedding gift is very common. Yu means "fish" and also "great wealth" in Mandarin so this gift also wishes prosperity for the couple.

- **The Golden Wheel**—This signifies the highest form of happiness and enlightenment.

- **The Lotus**—The lotus as it rises from the earth indicates that beauty and purity can rise from the most troubled of circumstances.

- **The Mystical Knot**—The knot generally has eight loops and is thought to bring happiness and personal possessions. It represents Buddha's endless wisdom and compassion.

- **The Right-Turning Conch Shell**—Traditionally an amulet for brave warriors, this symbol was accorded great power to subdue those that would attack them and strike terror into the hearts of their enemies. A right-turning shell is the most sacred because it follows the moon, sun, and stars across the sky. If you want power and authority, make this your talisman.

- **The Treasure Vase**—Brings contentment and harmony to the owner. The larger the vase the better, though it's important that the vase not overwhelm the room.

- **The White Umbrella**—This is protective and is thought to bring high honor and accolades. The White Umbrella Goddess protects against black magic.

IRELAND

Bells. In Ireland, brides place bells on their wedding dresses, in their bouquets, or they wear them as jewelry for luck. Bells are also given as gifts and are rung during the ceremony. Stories say that the bells scare away bad spirits that want to break up the happy couple.

The Blarney Stone. People have come from far and wide to kiss the Blarney Stone, which will bring them luck. To receive this luck, you must climb to the top of Blarney Castle, lean back, and hold onto a railing so your lips can reach the stone.

ISRAEL

Hamsa. *Hamsa,* the "hand of God," is thought to protect the wearer from the evil eye and bring luck and happiness. The sign is often used as a tattoo or as a charm for a necklace or bracelet. It can be spelled *hamesh, chamsa,* or *khamsa,* depending on what country it's from. In the Islamic faith, it is known as the "hand of Fatima."

IVORY COAST

Adinkra. See entry under *Ghana.*

JAPAN

Breaking Bottles. It is considered lucky to accidentally break a bottle of alcohol and is said to increase profits for a bar. However, it must be an accident. Deliberately breaking a bottle of alcohol is said to have the opposite effect.

Daruma Dolls. Daruma is a symbol of Bodhidharma, considered the founder of Zen Buddhism in China. The daruma doll is very good luck and is one of the odder-looking auspicious signs, with its round body without arms or legs and its painted beard and mustache. They are made of papier-mâché and should be weighted on the bottom so that if the doll is pushed over it will right itself. To receive the good luck that this doll can bring, you should first make a worthy wish or set a measurable goal. While concentrating on your wish or goal, use a black pen to fill in the doll's right eye. Set the doll on a high shelf, making sure you can easily see it every day. Each time you see the doll you should concentrate on your wish or goal. When your wish comes true or you have achieved your goal, fill in the left eye with a black pen and write what the wish or goal was on the back of the daruma doll. Be sure to be thankful and grateful for the luck that has come your way. If your wish does not come true within one year, the doll should be taken to a Buddhist temple and burned.

Maneki-neko. In Japan, the maneki-neko cat is a lucky figurine with a beckoning arm that helps businesses become prosperous.

KENYA

Fingo. This Kenyan talisman is from the Mijikenda people in the Coast Province. It is traditionally hidden in the sacred forest, or *kaya*, and once placed it will protect that forest and everyone who lives there.

Omieri. According to Luo folklore, Omieri is a black African python that lives in Lake Victoria and brings good luck in the form of summoning rain in times of drought.

NIGERIA

Eshu. If someone has a little bad luck, in Nigeria it is sometimes blamed on Eshu, a messenger of the gods who is also a bit of a trickster. There are many folk stories describing Eshu's antics.

PERU

Tumis. In Peru, the Tumi is a ceremonial knife that people often hang on their walls to ensure good luck in their homes.

POLAND

Carp Scales. In Poland, carp is traditionally served on Christmas day, and when the meal is over, the scales of the fish are saved and kept in a person's wallet as lucky talismans until the next Christmas Eve.

RUSSIA

Bird Droppings. In this country, if a bird poops on you, it's actually good luck and money will be coming your way. The more bird poop, the more money! It's considered lucky in Italy as well.

SERBIA

Spilling Water. It is a Serbian tradition to give good luck to someone who might be going on a trip, taking a test, or doing anything that might require a little extra positivity by spilling water behind them.

TURKEY

The Eye. In Turkey, locals often wear an eye-shaped talisman, usually made of glass with dark blue, light blue, black, and white concentric rings. It is meant to scare away the evil eye. This is a common symbol and can be seen throughout the Middle East and Eastern Europe.

UNITED KINGDOM

Chimney Sweeps. At first look, this is an odd bearer of luck, but the story here is that one day, King George II was riding his horse among his subjects when a dog ran in front of him and spooked the animal. As the horse reared, the king was nearly thrown from it, but a lowly chimney sweep saved the day when he stepped into the street and caught the halter, calmed the animal, and rescued the king from serious injury or even death.

Rabbit. In the United Kingdom, it's said that on the first day of the month, if you say the word "rabbit" when you wake up, before you say anything else, you will receive good luck for the rest of the month.

Spotted Dogs. If you meet a spotted dog or a black-and-white dog on your way to a business meeting, it's considered lucky.

UNITED STATES

Alligator Teeth. These are thought to give gamblers good luck and are often worn as necklaces or included in a mojo bag. Other items that are also supposed to bring success at the gambling tables or with the lottery

include rattlesnake rattles, rabbit's feet, buckeye nuts, and lucky hand root, also called salep root, which is hand shaped (hence the name) and comes from a wild orchid. These forms of luck have their origins in West Africa but are mostly practiced today by those in the American South.

Hex Signs. The Pennsylvania Dutch painted colorful six-sided geometric symbols on their barns that were commonly known as "hex" signs. They were supposed to give farmers and their families good luck. As the years went by, the shapes were simplified and today are often a five-sided shape called an "Amish barn star." These stars are often made of metal or wood, and they are prolific today, though most use them for aesthetic purposes.

Kachinas. Within the Pueblo, Hopi, and Zuni cultures in the American Southwest, Kachinas are symbols of individual native spirits. They are used equally in ceremonies and as playthings for children, and the dolls are thought to bring luck if one invites the spirit represented by a particular doll into the family.

URUGUAY

Throwing Water. In Uruguay, people throw water out their windows on New Year's Eve as a way to get rid of bad energy and start the new year off fresh.

VENEZUELA

Grapes. See entry under *Argentina*.

CHAPTER 6

SUPERSTITIONS

SUPERSTITION IN EVERYDAY LIFE

There are many ways to try turn your luck and avoid the evil eye. Superstitious people keep an eye out for certain signs that foretell good or bad luck in an effort to control their fate. Who's to say whether it works or not, but the peace of mind may be worth the effort.

* In card games and gambling, the idea of beginner's luck holds sway. Just by being new to the activity, the players gets a little extra luck on their side.

* In the United States, finding a penny on the ground is considered good luck. But the truly superstitious will only pick it up if it's facing heads up. If it's tails side up, turn it over and leave for another person to find in order to gain the luck.

* Three is a lucky number in many cases, but there's also the superstition that bad luck comes in threes. But once the third unlucky event has happened, you can breathe a sigh of relief that the worst is past.

* The cracks in a sidewalk or tile pattern can be hard to avoid, but if you step around them you may just

earn yourself a little extra luck. Or at least, that's the superstition.

❖ Be cautious the next time you make a toast. If you don't look people in the eye as you clink your glasses together, you'll be in for a round of bad luck. If you believe that sort of thing, that is.

❖ There's potential luck in everything, but once you find a lucky item, you want to replicate that experience. That's what gives rise to lucky shirts, lucky underwear, or even lucky hairstyles to help make your desired outcome come true. If it works once, it has to work every time. Right?

SUPERSTITIONS ON THE SEA

Those that turn to the sea, regardless of nationality, have many superstitions that have held on from the times when sailing around the world was a dangerous business.

- Calling a sailor Jonah means you think they embody bad luck, and sailors of yore would do their best to avoid these men.

- Just like traveling, sailing on a Friday is best avoided.

- If, while sailing, a crew member sees an albatross, it's good luck. The poem "The Rime of the Ancient Mariner" originated the phrase "like an albatross around my neck" which describes someone experiencing an annoying run of bad luck.

- Bananas are bad luck, and private boats or fishing yachts will avoid carrying them on board.

- Whistle on board and a storm will challenge the ship.

- Many ships carried cats on board for a variety of reasons, particularly because they would catch rats and other pests on the ship. But sailors also thought they provided good luck in the form of protection from bad weather, though they would avoid saying the word "cat." Black cats were particularly favored. Sailor's wives would keep black cats to ensure that their husbands would return from the sea. Some crew members even thought that cats had magic stored in their tails and could actually start a storm if they chose. So as you might imagine, cats were very well treated on their seafaring journeys.

SUPERSTITION IN SPORTS

BASEBALL

Athletes and sports fans are a superstitious lot, and once they find an item or ritual that might help their team win, they'll keep it up until it stops working. Here are a selection of superstitions from athletes of all kinds.

❖ Baseball players are so superstitious that they are superstitious about being superstitious and often won't even talk about it.

❖ Before he retired, Nomar Garciaparra had many rituals he followed, including adjusting the Velcro on his gloves repeatedly and tapping his toes before every pitch. He also kissed his bat before getting in the on-deck circle and would not let anyone touch his hat.

❖ Elliot Johnson always chews grape-flavored Super Bubble gum when he plays defense on the field, but when he's hitting he switches to watermelon flavor.

- Baseball fans will turn their hats inside out if their team is in danger of losing.

- Former pitcher Scott Erickson would wear only black on the days that he pitched, and he would refuse to speak to anyone.

- Steve Kline never washed his hat for the entire season. Many other players observe the same superstition.

- Wade Boggs ate chicken before every game, and his wife became so used to this that she had more than forty different recipes for chicken. Together, they authored a cookbook called *Fowl Tips*.

- Some players spit on their hands before picking up the bat.

- No one talks to a pitcher who is in the middle of a no-hitter.

- Pitchers sometimes don't shave on a game day.

- If a player has a good day of hitting, they will continue to use the same bat until the streak wears off.

- Some players try sleeping with their bat to break a bad hitting streak.

- Don't step on the foul lines when you are running on or off the field.

- Before leaving the field, many players step on one of the bases. Joe DiMaggio always stepped on second base before leaving the field.

- Before the game starts, some players stick a chewed piece of gum on their hat.

- Never let a dog walk across the diamond before the game starts.

- Never lend your bat to another player.

BASKETBALL

- College coach Jerry Tarkanian would chew a towel during games.

- Michael Jordan always wore his UNC (University of North Carolina) shorts under his NBA shorts during games.

- Caron Butler once obsessively drank Mountain Dew before and during games. He switched to chewing on straws after the National Basketball Players Association banned him from drinking while playing, but eventually the NBA even banned his new ritual.

- Mike Bibby clips his nails during time-outs.

- The last person to shoot a basket at practice will have a good game that day.

- The night before every game, Jason Terry sleeps in the team shorts of his opponent. He has a pair for every team in the league.

- Bounce the ball a few times before taking a foul shot.

- Before a game, wipe the soles of your basketball shoes to ensure good luck.

BOWLING

❖ If you are on a winning streak, be sure to wear the same clothes every time you play until you lose.

❖ A perfect score in bowling is three hundred, so that number is lucky and is often used on license plates to increase a player's chances of winning.

❖ Players often keep charms in their pockets or bowling ball bags to increase their luck.

FISHING

❖ Be sure to throw back the first fish you catch, otherwise it's unlikely that you'll catch another for the rest of the day.

❖ Use the same rod for the entire day or bad luck will follow.

❖ Some fishermen spit on their bait before casting. They think the fish will bite better.

❖ Others believe that you won't catch any fish if you pass a barefooted woman on your way to the boat.

FOOTBALL

* Bears linebacker Brian Urlacher would eat two chocolate chip cookies before every game.

* College coach Les Miles actually eats a little of the field before every game.

* Double numbers on a player's jersey are lucky, which is why you see such high numbers in football, as opposed to other sports like baseball.

* For optimum luck, players should keep their number even if they are traded to another team.

* Mascots are thought to be very lucky for their teams.

GOLF

* Players often carry a few coins in their pocket as a good luck charm.

* Use an odd-numbered club for your first shot.

* Don't use a ball with a number higher than four—that's very bad luck.

HOCKEY

- ❖ The great Wayne Gretzky would put on his uniform in the same order for every game. He also put baby powder on his stick before the first face-off.

- ❖ Ed Belfour would not let anyone touch any of this gear.

- ❖ Pelle Lindbergh had a whole bunch of rituals he would follow for games including drinking a Pripps beer between each period, which had to be served by the same assistant coach every time, and the glass had to have two ice cubes in it. He also wore the same orange shirt under his protective padding for every game, and by the end of his career it was falling apart.

NASCAR

- ❖ Green cars are considered bad luck.

- ❖ Drivers won't carry fifty-dollar bills; it's considered bad luck.

❖ No peanut shells are allowed on the track. You can eat peanuts and have other peanut products, but no shells. Years ago, peanut shells were found in a few wrecks where the drivers had died.

❖ Some drivers always enter their cars from one particular side.

SOCCER

❖ Cristiano Ronaldo needs to the be the first player to leave the plane if the team has to fly to a game. He also needs to step onto the field with his right foot first every time.

❖ Back in 1969, Dutch player Johan Cruyff didn't follow his usual habit of spitting his chewing gum toward the opposing goal in one game, and they were soundly beaten that day.

❖ During the 1998 World Cup, French player Laurent Blanc would kiss the shaved head of goalkeeper Fabien Barthez before each game for luck. The whole team also listened to Gloria Gaynor's "I Will Survive" in the locker room before every match.

- The Australian team, the Socceroos, was a losing team until 1969, when they had a witch doctor put a curse on the Rhodesian team before a playoff match in Mozambique. They won the game, but when the witch doctor asked to be paid, the Australians didn't have enough money. The witch doctor reversed the curse and the Socceroos started losing games again. The curse remained until 2004 when comedian John Safran broke it by going back to Mozambique and the stadium where that game in 1969 was played, along with a new witch doctor who killed a chicken and spread its blood on the field. After, Safran and one of the original Australian players, Johnny Warren, washed themselves at the Australian team stadium with clay provided by the witch doctor. Extreme, yes, but the curse was lifted and the Socceroos went on to have a winning 2006 season.

- Mia Hamm always crossed her right shoelace over her left and if she didn't, she got very anxious.

- During the World Cup in 1962, the Chilean team would eat or drink the stereotypical food or drink of the opposing country (spaghetti when playing Italy, vodka when playing Russia, for example).

* Striker Javier Hernández prays on his knees on the pitch before each game.

* Luis Suárez of Uruguay kisses the tattoo of his daughter's name on his wrist for good luck.

TENNIS

* Serena Williams wears the same pair of socks throughout an entire tournament. She also bounces the ball five times before her first serve and two times before her second serve.

* Rafael Nadal has many rituals that he thinks help him focus on his game including holding his racket with one hand while walking onto the court and making sure that his tournament ID tag is always facing up on his equipment bag.

* Andre Agassi would send his rackets to tournaments in a separate vehicle.

* It's bad luck to step on the lines on the court.

❖ Many players eat at one restaurant before every tournament. It's common for them to eat the same meal at the restaurant as well.

❖ At Wimbledon, Björn Borg would never shave, so he would start the tournament clean shaven and by the end, he would look pretty shaggy.

SUPERSTITION IN THE THEATER

Another notoriously superstitious group, those who work in the theater have many rituals and rules to keep bad luck from the stage.

* In the early days of theater, it was expensive to create the color blue to dye clothing, so it was not used very much. As time went by, it became bad luck to wear blue in the theater unless you wear silver at the same time.

* Light in general is not bad luck, but it is considered bad to have three candles grouped together on a stage, and some people think that the person closest to the shortest candle might be the next to die.

* Disaster will befall any production that has peacock feathers onstage for any purpose, whether it's sewn into a costume or part of the set.

* It has become tradition to give a bouquet of flowers stolen from a graveyard to the director or the leading lady. However, this is done only on closing night to symbolize the end of the production.

- It's bad luck for mirrors to be used onstage, though this may be a technical requirement to avoid unfortunate reflections that detract from the performance.

- According to Aristotle, Thespis was the first actor to speak onstage playing a character, and today some think that he haunts theaters. To keep his antics at bay, they give him one night of his own when the theater will remain empty. This is generally on a Monday and it is the traditional night off for theater folk.

- Some think at least one light should always be burning in a theater to scare away ghosts.

- It is very bad luck to whistle in a theater and it signals that someone will soon be fired. This had practical origins; in the early days of theater, coded whistles were used to cue actors when to go onstage. Any noncoded whistling would confuse them and cause them to miss their cues or otherwise disrupt the performance.

- It's bad luck to wish someone good luck in the theater. Suggesting an actor "break a leg" is now the accepted way to wish actors good luck. There are many stories explaining the origins of "break a leg," and most refer to actors bowing at the end of a show at which time they would bend their leg or "break" the line of the leg.

* Never say *Macbeth* in a theater or bad luck will follow the production. This goes back to Shakespeare himself, who allegedly put a curse on the play so that no one would be able to successfully direct it except for him. But the word itself is avoided in any theater and for any play.

CHAPTER 7

BAD LUCK AND HOW TO AVOID IT

AVOIDING BAD LUCK

Here's a list of things that are best avoided if you want to keep luck on your side.

❖ Don't open an umbrella inside. There are many stories about why this is bad luck. One is that a woman in Rome opened her umbrella inside and her house collapsed soon thereafter. But most accounts believe it's just common sense to wait until you leave the house to open it—you don't want to poke someone's eye out.

* Don't walk under a ladder. This one is unlucky for a couple of reasons. First, it's generally dangerous to walk under a ladder—there may be someone working above who could fall or drop something onto your head. However, it also has religious connotations. A leaning ladder forms a triangle which is interpreted as the Holy Trinity. Those who break that trinity by walking under the ladder may have been seen as blasphemous.

* Don't enter a building with your left foot first. When you enter someone's home for the first time, you must start with your right foot, which will bring luck to the home and all who live in it. This is also part of a New Year's tradition. The story goes that a child needs to smash a pomegranate on the front step of a home. The first person to enter the home after midnight must step over the pulp and enter the building with their right foot. This will bring luck to the household for the upcoming year.

* Don't darn a pair of socks for your sweetheart or your sweetheart'll soon leave you forever.

* Don't dress your left arm or leg first. It's generally thought that doing anything with your right appendage first is lucky, and your left unlucky. So, think

carefully as you put on your clothes to achieve maximum good luck.

❖ Don't break a mirror. In days of yore, people thought mirrors held pieces of your soul inside them. The conventional wisdom is that if you break a mirror, you'll have seven years bad luck.

❖ Don't enter and leave a home using different doors. It is particularly unlucky for a bride and groom to enter by one door and leave by another, but it's an inauspicious act for anyone. It's also unlucky to enter a home by the back door.

❖ Don't look at your own doppelganger. Some think a doppelganger—the physical double of another person—is an evil twin and should be avoided at all costs. If your family or friends see a person who looks just like you, it's said that bad luck may follow.

❖ Don't spit. Do this in public and it may land on an invisible spirit who will then curse you. But maybe do, since in some cultures, spitting is used to ward off evil.

❖ Don't stir tea counterclockwise. In years gone by, many thought that going in any direction counter to the sun was unlucky. The sun was thought to move clockwise so any counterclockwise movement is not auspicious.

❖ Don't let a black cat cross your path. Black cats aren't a universally unlucky symbol, but they are considered bad luck in a number of cultures around the world. And even in places where they are considered good luck, it's still not good to have them cross your path from right to left. Instead of having to remember all the details, do yourself a favor and avoid having a black cat cross your path at all. Then you don't have to worry about whether you've just invited bad luck.

CURSES, TABOOS, AND
BAD OMENS

EVIL EYE

In more ancient times, giving someone the evil eye was serious business and was thought to be the source of both physical and mental illnesses. There are a variety of talismans and amulets to wear or keep in your pocket to ward off any curses sent your way via the evil eye. An object showing a hand with an eye in the center is the choice of some cultures. In other countries, all you need are beads in blue or green.

LAUGHING

In general, laughing is not a bad thing, but if you laugh before breakfast, the story is that you'll be crying before supper. And excessive laughing is a sign that you are possessed and that you'll die soon.

MIRRORS

Don't place a mirror directly facing your bed. This is to avoid having your spirit leave your body and get stuck in the mirror, never able to return.

OWLS

In North America and Europe, barn owls are thought to be a bad omen because of their ability to fly silently. Some poets of the eighteenth and nineteenth centuries used owls to symbolize impending doom. In other cultures, the screech of an owl is also a harbinger of death.

PEACOCKS

It's thought that the feathers of peacocks are unlucky because they look like eyes—the evil eye, specifically—and that they would bring bad luck to you and your family if you brought them into your home.

RAVENS

In the United Kingdom, many believe that if ravens leave the Tower of London, disaster will follow. Even today, ravens are kept in the tower and their wings are clipped to prevent them from flying away.

WHISTLING

Avoid whistling at night or wandering spirits might follow you home.

THE WRYNECK OR JINX TORQUILLA

This is a type of bird that can twist its head around almost 180 degrees. There is a superstition that says if they turn their heads and point them at you there is a death coming in your future. The word "jinx" is derived from this bird.

YAWNING

Be sure to cover your mouth with your hand to avoid evil spirits from entering your body.

Good luck!